BY SLOANE GOULD

VISIT AMERICA'S NATIONAL PARKS!

VISIT

JOSHUA TREE NATIONAL PARK!

Enslow PUBLISHING

Please visit our website, www.enslow.com. For a free color catalog of all our high-quality books, call toll free 1-800-398-2504 or fax 1-877-980-4454.

Library of Congress Cataloging-in-Publication Data
Names: Gould, Sloane, author.
Title: Visit Joshua Tree National Park! / Sloane Gould.
Description: Buffalo, NY : Enslow Publishing, [2026] | Series: Visit America's national parks! | Includes bibliographical references and index.
Identifiers: LCCN 2024058613 (print) | LCCN 2024058614 (ebook) | ISBN 9781978544192 (library binding) | ISBN 9781978544185 (paperback) | ISBN 9781978544208 (ebook)
Subjects: LCSH: Joshua Tree National Park (Calif.)–Juvenile literature.
Classification: LCC F868.J6 G68 2026 (print) | LCC F868.J6 (ebook) | DDC 917.94/9704–dc23/eng/20250203
LC record available at https://lccn.loc.gov/2024058613
LC ebook record available at https://lccn.loc.gov/2024058614

Published in 2026 by
Enslow Publishing
2544 Clinton Street
Buffalo, NY 14224

Designer: Tanya Dellaccio Keeney
Editor: Caitie McAneney

Photo credits: Cover (background) VIKVAD/Shutterstock.com; cover (illustration) ideapaad66/Shutterstock.com; p. 5 (sign) CL Shebley/Shutterstock.com; p. 5 (tree) Amanda Sala/Shutterstock.com; p. 6/7 (mural) Joshua Tree National Park/Flickr.com; p. 7 (cactus) Studio Barcelona/Shutterstock.com; p. 9 AndrePagaPhoto/Shutterstock.com; p. 10 Diane N. Ennis/Shutterstock.com; p. 11 Julija Sulkovska/Shutterstock.com; p. 13 Anastasia _ Photography/Shutterstock.com; p. 15 Aquila Art Work/Shutterstock.com; p. 17 (roadrunner) Milan Sommer/Shutterstock.com; p. 17 (kangaroo rat) Nicholas Taffs/Shutterstock.com; p. 19 Greg Epperson/Shutterstock.com; p. 21 thomaslabriekl/Shutterstock.com.

Printed in the United States of America

CPSIA compliance information: Batch #CSENS26: For further information contact Enslow Publishing at 1-800-398-2504.

CONTENTS

Words in the glossary appear in **bold** type the first time they are used in the text.

A DESERT DELIGHT

Have you ever wanted to explore the rich **ecosystem** within a desert? Joshua Tree National Park gives visitors a once-in-a-lifetime desert adventure.

Joshua Tree National Park is a park in Southern California. It's the meeting place of the Mojave Desert and the Sonoran Desert. Though they're both deserts, they are totally different in temperature, wildlife, and **vegetation**. Because of its cool rock **formations**, this national park is a favorite spot for hikers and rock climbers.

Joshua trees are tall, twisted trees with spiky leaves and white flowers.

MORE TO KNOW

More than 1.3 million people visit Joshua Tree National Park each year.

PARK HISTORY

People have lived on the land that makes up Joshua Tree National Park for more than 10,000 years. In the 1920s, people started to travel on roads through the desert. Some people came to steal cacti.

Activist Minerva Hoyt worked to **protect** desert lands. She thought desert plants such as cacti were important. President Franklin Delano Roosevelt listened to her. He made the area Joshua Tree National Monument in 1936.

This mural, or large painting, of Minerva Hoyt is at the visitor center in Joshua Tree National Park.

MORE TO KNOW

In 1994, Joshua Tree National Monument became a national park.

AMAZING MOJAVE

The Mojave Desert takes up the western part of Joshua Tree National Park. Joshua trees grow throughout this part of the park. It's considered the "high desert," as it is above 3,000 feet (914.4 m) in **elevation**.

Less than 5 inches (12.7 cm) of rain fall in the Mojave Desert each year. There's more vegetation in this desert than in the Sonoran Desert. The temperatures in the Mojave Desert are cooler than in the Sonoran Desert.

MORE TO KNOW

North America has four deserts. The Mojave Desert is the smallest of them all.

These huge rock formations are in the Mojave part of Joshua Tree.

SUPER SONORAN

The Sonoran Desert is in the southwestern United States and northern Mexico. The western part of it is called the Colorado. This is the part that you'll visit in Joshua Tree National Park.

This part of the park is the "low desert" because it has a lower elevation than the Mojave Desert. Much of it is hot, flat, and rocky. A few kinds of plants call this place home, including the cholla cactus and thorny plants called ocotillos.

OCOTILLO

MORE TO KNOW

The Colorado Desert is the most arid, or dry, part of North America.

Many people visit the Cholla Cactus Garden in the Sonoran part of Joshua Tree National Park.

WHAT'S THE WEATHER?

Desert weather is often hot and dry. However, temperature changes throughout the year. Many people like to visit in fall or spring. The temperature usually climbs to around 85°F (29.4°C) during the day.

In the winter, weather is cooler at around 60°F (15.5 °C). You will probably want to wear a jacket if you visit. At night, it can be freezing. In the summer, you can skip the jacket, as temperatures soar above 100°F (37.8 °C)!

MORE TO KNOW

Some higher elevations of the park get snow in the winter!

Daytime is much warmer in the desert than nighttime. If you go on a long hike, bring **layers** of clothing.

AWESOME ATTRACTIONS

What kinds of **attractions** draw visitors to this park? Many people like to visit the beautiful Cholla Cactus Garden. Others want to see Skull Rock, a huge rock worn down by **erosion**, making it look like a skull.

Joshua Tree's many nature trails are the perfect way to explore the park. Many people hike the Hidden Valley Nature Trail and Barker Dam Nature Trail. Others hike to the Cottonwood Springs Oasis, which is a perfect place for birdwatching.

MORE TO KNOW

An oasis is spot in the desert where water and vegetation are found.

Cottonwood Springs Oasis has a natural spring, or flow of water, that has been used for hundreds of years.

WILDLIFE WATCH

You might think that deserts don't have many animals. But Joshua Tree National Park is a great place for wildlife lovers! More than 50 species, or kinds, of mammals live in the park, including kangaroo rats and bobcats. More than 40 species of reptiles are found here as well, including rattlesnakes and lizards.

More than 700 species of plants can be found in the park. Many of them have poisons and spikes for protection. Cacti store water in their thick stems to survive.

Birds such as roadrunners also live in Joshua Tree National Park.

MORE TO KNOW

Kangaroo rats are great desert animals. They barely need any water to live!

KANGAROO RAT

CLIMBING AND BOULDERING

People can explore Joshua Tree National Park by foot, car, horse, or bike. Many people also like to climb the many mountains, rock piles, and boulders there. This park offers more than 8,000 climbing **routes**!

Many climbers enjoy climbing a large rock formation called The Great Burrito. This rock formation has many natural cracks that help climbers make their way up to the top. There are climbs for people of all levels within the park.

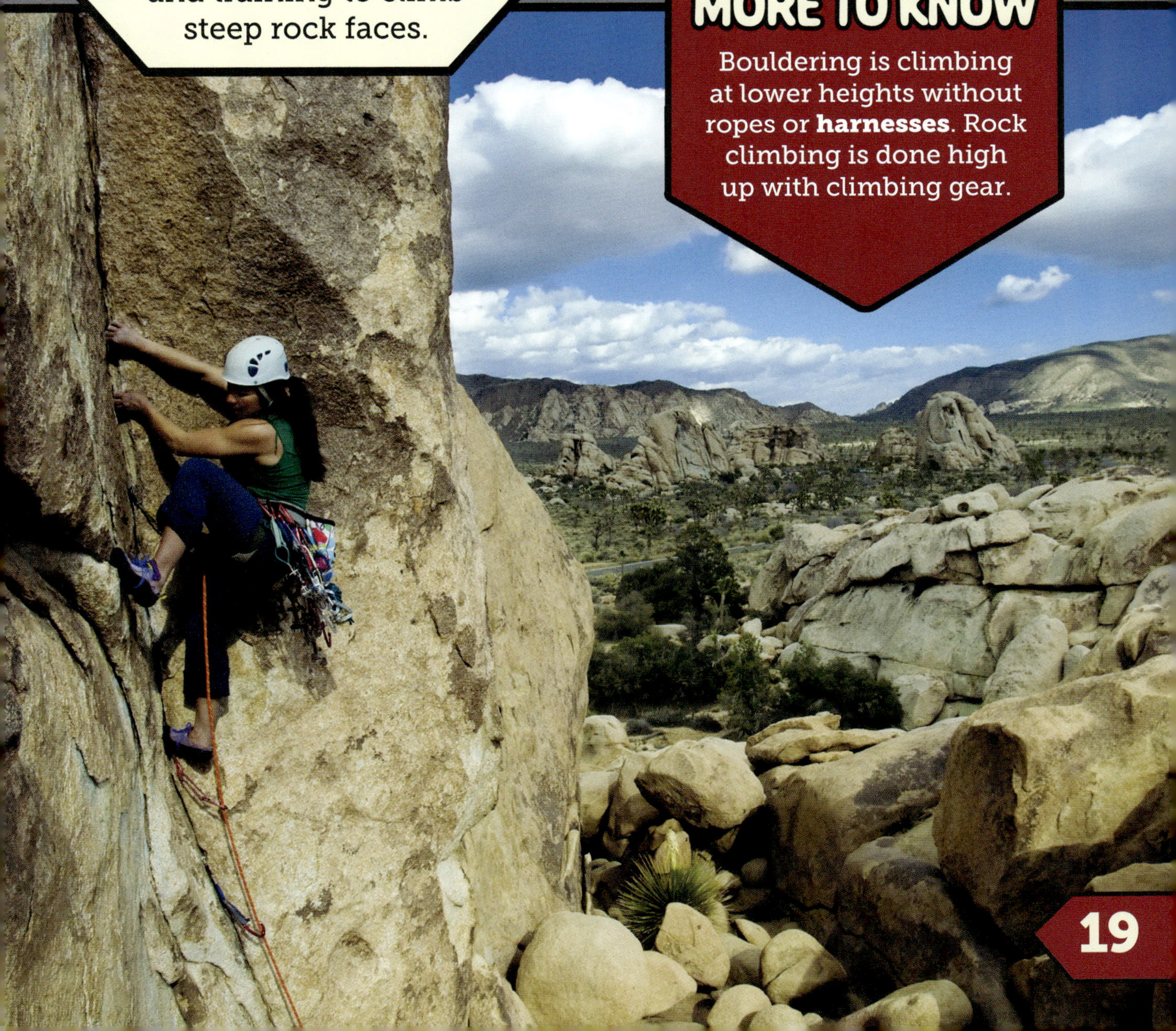

You need special gear and training to climb steep rock faces.

MORE TO KNOW

Bouldering is climbing at lower heights without ropes or **harnesses**. Rock climbing is done high up with climbing gear.

EXPLORE JOSHUA TREE!

Joshua Tree National Park is a special place full of one-of-a-kind ecosystems and rock formations. It's home to wildlife and plants that are made to survive the hot days, cold nights, and little rain of the desert.

You can explore the park during any season. There are around 500 places to camp in the park if you'd like to catch a desert sunrise. Rock formations made by years of erosion make this park a sight to see!

MORE TO KNOW

Many birds stop in Joshua Tree National Park while migrating, or moving from place to place.

Rain and wind wore away at rocks to make arches like this one.

GLOSSARY

activist: Someone who acts strongly in support of or against an issue.

attraction: Something people travel to see.

ecosystem: A natural community of life that includes living and nonliving features.

elevation: Height above sea level.

erosion: The physical process in which soil and rock is moved by wind or water.

formation: One unit of rocks made up of a bed of rocks or a series of beds.

harness: A set of straps fitted to a person to keep them in place or safe from falling.

layer: Something lying over or under another thing.

protect: To keep safe.

route: A way to get from one place to another.

vegetation: Trees, bushes, and other plants.

FOR MORE INFORMATION

Books

Culliford, Amy. *Desert Animal Habitats*. St. Catharines, Ontario, Canada: Crabtree Publishing, 2025.

Kuo Lee, Jean. *California*. Minneapolis, MN: Kids Core, 2025.

Websites

Desert Habitat
kids.nationalgeographic.com/nature/habitats/article/desert
Explore fun facts about desert habitats with National Geographic Kids.

Kangaroo Rat
www.nps.gov/orpi/learn/nature/kangaroo-rat.htm
Learn more about the kangaroo rats that call Joshua Tree National Park home.

Publisher's note to educators and parents: Our editors have carefully reviewed these websites to ensure that they are suitable for students. Many websites change frequently, however, and we cannot guarantee that a site's future contents will continue to meet our high standards of quality and educational value. Be advised that students should be closely supervised whenever they access the internet.

INDEX